Simple Machine Science

Pulleys

By Madison Miller

Gareth Stevens
Publishing

Please visit our website, www.garethstevens.com. For a free color catalog of all our high-quality books, call toll free 1-800-542-2595 or fax 1-877-542-2596.

Library of Congress Cataloging-in-Publication Data

Miller, Madison, author.
 Pulleys / Madison Miller.
  pages cm. — (Simple machine science)
 Includes bibliographical references and index.
 ISBN 978-1-4339-8142-5 (paperback)
 ISBN 978-1-4339-8143-2 (6-pack)
 ISBN 978-1-4339-8141-8 (library binding)
 1. Pulleys—Juvenile literature. I. Title.
 TJ1103.M55 2013
 621.8—dc23

2012020376

Published in 2013 by
Gareth Stevens Publishing
111 East 14th Street, Suite 349
New York, NY 10003

Copyright © 2013 Gareth Stevens Publishing

Designer: Katelyn E. Reynolds
Editor: Greg Roza

Photo credits: Cover, pp. 1, 9 iStockphoto/Thinkstock.com; pp. 3–24 (background graphics) mike.irwin/Shutterstock.com; p. 5 Comstock/Thinkstock.com; p. 7 © iStockphoto.com/creisinger; p. 11 Michael Shake/Shutterstock.com; p. 13 aragami12345s/Shutterstock.com; p. 15 Andrew McDonough/Shutterstock.com; p. 17 Rikard Stadler/Shutterstock.com; p. 19 SergeyIT/Shutterstock.com; p. 21 ppl/Shutterstock.com.

All rights reserved. No part of this book may be reproduced in any form without permission in writing from the publisher, except by a reviewer.

Printed in the United States of America

CPSIA compliance information: Batch #CW13GS: For further information contact Gareth Stevens, New York, New York at 1-800-542-2595.

Contents

Into the Groove 4
Change Direction 6
Out to Dry 8
Belts and Pulleys 10
Heavy Lifting 12
Block and Tackle 14
What's a Winch? 18
Get a Lift from Pulleys 20
Glossary 22
For More Information 23
Index 24

Boldface words appear in the glossary.

Into the Groove

A pulley is a special wheel used to do work. It has a **groove** around the outer edge. A rope or cable fits into the groove. The groove keeps the rope or cable from slipping off the pulley.

5

Change Direction

Pulleys are used to change the direction of a pulling force. This lets us lift something up by pulling down on a rope. Flagpoles use pulleys. When you pull down on the rope, the flag goes up.

← pulley

7

Out to Dry

Have you ever seen shirts hanging on a clothesline between two buildings? This type of clothesline uses two pulleys to change the direction of a pulling force. When you pull the rope toward you, the clothes go away from you.

9

Belts and Pulleys

Some machines use belts and pulleys. A belt is like a rope with the ends joined together. When one pulley turns, it moves a belt. The belt then turns other pulleys. Cars use belts to turn more than one pulley.

11

Heavy Lifting

We also use pulleys to lift heavy loads. Sometimes all we need is a **fixed** pulley. Other times, we use fixed and movable pulleys together. The more pulleys there are, the less effort is needed to lift something.

← **fixed pulley**

← **movable pulley**

13

Block and Tackle

A block and tackle is a special pulley system. A block is two or more pulleys on one **axle**. Two blocks with a rope around their pulleys are a tackle. A block and tackle uses many pulleys to make lifting a load easier.

15

You may have seen block and tackles on ships. They're used to raise heavy sails. Big ships need big block and tackles. The more pulleys a block and tackle has, the longer the rope needs to be.

17

What's a Winch?

A winch is used to pull in and let out a rope. Some are moved by hand. Some are moved by machines. Winches and pulleys work together to lift heavy loads. Elevators use winches and pulleys. So do cranes.

19

Get a Lift from Pulleys

Do you like skiing? If you do, you've likely used a **chairlift**. Chairlifts use pulleys to keep the seats moving smoothly. Two pulleys on each end of the lift change the direction the seats move.

Pulleys in Our World

flagpole   clothesline   car belt
ship and sail   elevator   crane   chairlift

21

Glossary

axle: the bar on which a wheel turns

chairlift: a machine that carries skiers up and down a mountain

fixed: not moving

groove: a narrow space cut into something

For More Information

Books
Bodden, Valerie. *Pulleys*. Mankato, MN: Creative Education, 2011.

Dahl, Michael. *Pull, Lift, and Lower: A Book About Pulleys*. Minneapolis, MN: Picture Window Books, 2006.

Smith, Siân. *Pulleys*. Chicago, IL: Heinemann Library, 2013.

Websites

Flag Raiser
www.education.com/science-fair/article/flag-raiser/
Learn more about fixed pulleys with two simple activities.

Simple Machines
www.msichicago.org/fileadmin/Activities/Games/simple_machines/
Learn more about pulleys and other simple machines by playing a fun online game.

Publisher's note to educators and parents: Our editors have carefully reviewed these websites to ensure that they are suitable for students. Many websites change frequently, however, and we cannot guarantee that a site's future contents will continue to meet our high standards of quality and educational value. Be advised that students should be closely supervised whenever they access the Internet.

Index

axle 14

belts 10, 21

block and tackle 14, 16

cable 4

cars 10, 21

chairlifts 20, 21

clothesline 8, 21

cranes 18, 21

elevators 18, 21

fixed pulley 12

flagpoles 6, 21

groove 4

loads 12, 14, 18

movable pulley 12

pulling force 6, 8

rope 4, 6, 8, 10, 14, 16, 18

sails 16, 21

ships 16, 21

winch 18